Robert E. Lee

Robert E. Lee

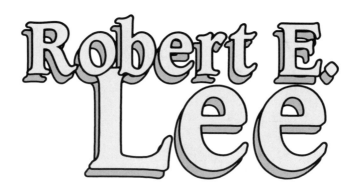

Nathan Aaseng

Lerner Publications Company • Minneapolis

Photographs and illustrations courtesy of Independent Picture Service, pp. 2, 9, 28, 63; Virginia State Library and Archives, pp. 6, 15, 24 (top), 37, 46, 54, 100, 103 (both), 106; Georgia Department of Archives and History, p. 10; Robert E. Lee Memorial Association, p. 12 (both); National Gallery of Art, p. 16; Washington and Lee University, pp. 22, 24 (bottom), 104; Library of Congress, pp. 32, 40, 42, 47, 49 (bottom), 52, 61 (top), 64, 66, 68, 71, 72, 73, 77, 78, 79, 81, 85, 87, 94; Chicago Historical Society, pp. 34, 49 (top), 50; National Archives, pp. 39, 57, 61 (bottom), 88, 92, 95, 97.

Front cover painting: Robert E. Lee Memorial Association. Additional illustration by Darren Erickson. Back cover photograph: Independent Picture Service.

Maps on pages 31, 45, and 58 by Laura Westlund.

Library of Congress Cataloging-in-Publication Data

Aaseng, Nathan.
  Robert E. Lee / Nathan Aaseng.
      p.   cm.
  Includes bibliographical references and index.
  Summary: Biography of the brilliant and daring commander of Confederate forces during the Civil War. Reviews his campaigns and strategies, and his strengths and weaknesses as a leader.
  ISBN 0-8225-4909-3 (lib. bdg.)
  1. Lee, Robert E. (Robert Edward), 1807-1870—Juvenile literature.
2. Generals—United States—Biography—Juvenile literature.
3. Confederate States of America. Army—Biography—Juvenile literature. 4. United States. Army—Biography—Juvenile literature. 5. United States—History—Civil War, 1861-1865—Campaigns—Juvenile literature. [1. Lee, Robert E. (Robert Edward), 1807-1870. 2. Generals.] I. Title.
E467.1.L4A15   1991
[92]—dc20   90-45884
                                                                          CIP
                                                                          AC

Manufactured in the United States of America

1 2 3 4 5 6 7 8 9 10 00 99 98 97 96 95 94 93 92 91

Contents

ONE

A Living Legend

Throughout the summer of 1862, the Army of Northern Virginia had thoroughly baffled the Union forces in the Civil War. The Army of Northern Virginia was fighting for the Confederate States of America, a group of 11 Southern states that had seceded, or withdrawn, from the United States. The federal, or Union, armies were made up of Northerners who were fighting to keep the states together in one country.

With bold strategies, brilliant deception, and swift anticipation of the opponent's moves, the Army of Northern Virginia had driven the Federals from the outskirts of Richmond, Virginia, and had sent them scuttling back to protect their own capital, Washington, D.C. The Confederate army, under the command of General Robert E. Lee, disappeared and reappeared so eerily that it shattered the confidence of one Union general after another.

In September, Robert E. Lee's bold campaign was halted by misfortune. A misplaced copy of Lee's battle orders fell into enemy hands. With the aid of this information, the Union army of General George McClellan was able to stop the Confederate advance at Antietam Creek, Maryland, in the deadliest one-day battle ever fought in the United States.

After withdrawing his troops from Maryland back into Confederate territory, Lee was forced to replot his strategy. At the same time he was burdened with a new worry. One of his daughters, 23-year-old Annie, had become seriously ill while vacationing in North Carolina. The arrival of personal mail each day was laden with tension as Lee awaited the latest word on his daughter's condition.

One morning, a batch of mail was delivered to the tent that Lee used as his headquarters. The general looked over the correspondence and then summoned his aide, Walter Taylor. Were there any military matters that needed immediate attention? Lee asked. Taylor brought in the latest reports and waited while Lee carefully evaluated his army's needs and wrote out his orders. Taylor left to distribute the orders, but he returned a few minutes later.

He found Lee weeping, clutching a letter in his hands. The news of Annie's death had arrived with the earlier correspondence. Yet somehow Lee had choked back his deep anguish without giving his aide a clue as to what had happened. Only after he made sure that his army had been adequately taken care of did he permit himself to grieve.

Of all his attributes, perhaps it was this astounding self-control and devotion to duty that set Robert E. Lee apart as one of the most respected persons in military history.

True, Lee was a brilliant and daring military strategist. In the dashing tradition of his father, a Revolutionary War hero, he consistently outwitted his foes. When General Ulysses S. Grant took command of the Union forces after a string of successes in the West, the Northerners were so demoralized that they scoffed at Grant's optimism. "You haven't faced Bobby Lee yet," they repeated.

Yet it was not Lee's military tactics that inspired a starving Confederate army to keep fighting, even when the situation looked hopeless, and to hail Lee with a deafening cheer, even after he had been forced to surrender. It was not his genius that caused his opponents to treat him with respect bordering on awe, even when they defeated him. Rather it was his unswerving commitment to doing what he believed was right that won Robert E. Lee the admiration of his contemporaries and later generations.

Northern general Ulysses S. Grant forced Lee to surrender, but future generations would regard Lee as the greater hero.

Southern soldiers loved General Lee.

Lee was not the godlike "marble man" that some colleagues described, immune from all sins and shortcomings. He occasionally displayed such furious outbursts of temper that many of those who dealt with him on a day-to-day basis lived in fear of him. Lee could alternate from soft-hearted weakness (he seldom could bring himself to replace incompetent commanders) to righteous wrath (he once ordered a soldier shot for stealing a pig).

Until the Civil War, Lee's career had been a long series of frustrations that repeatedly sent him into deep depression. During the war, he proved capable of mistakes in strategy. Even after achieving fame as a general, he continued to wonder whether he had wasted his entire life in the wrong career. In some ways, Lee's marriage was a disappointment, and he was such a possessive father that he strongly encouraged his daughters not to marry (none of them did).

Despite these human frailties, Lee's devotion to duty never wavered. Loyalty to his native state of Virginia caused him to turn down the career opportunity of a lifetime—field command of the United States Army—and to join the Confederate cause. Virginia, like the other Confederate states, had left the Union over the issues of slavery and states' rights. Even though Lee did not believe in either slavery or the right of states to withdraw from the Union, he remained loyal to his home state.

As a leader, Lee praised his generals and his soldiers in victory and accepted all blame for failure. Commitment to religious principles led Lee to treat both civilians and enemies with compassion. When General Jubal Early angrily remarked that he wished all Northern soldiers were dead, Lee kindly stated, "How can you say so, General? Now, I wish they were all at home, attending to their own business, leaving us to do the same."

When the war was lost, Lee tried to set an example for the South of how to rebuild without bitterness. He took over the leadership of a tiny, failing college. There, he once threatened to resign if he ever heard a word of disrespect uttered about his former adversary, President Ulysses S. Grant.

Lee's reputation for greatness can best be summed up by a question once asked by a young Southerner: "Was General Lee in the Old Testament or the New Testament?" Even in his own time, Robert Edward Lee was something of a legend.

Henry Lee and the grand Stratford Hall, Robert's boyhood home

TWO

Crumbling Dynasty

1807-1829

Although Robert Edward Lee was born into the illustrious Lee family, one of the most highly respected families in the United States, he did not have a happy or carefree childhood. Perhaps Robert developed his great sense of self-control and responsibility because his father, Henry, lacked these traits.

The Lees of Virginia were already a prominent family when Henry Lee made a name for himself as one of the most daring officers of the American Revolution. "Light Horse Harry," as he became known, was a close friend and trusted advisor to General George Washington. Henry Lee seemed destined for greatness. He devised the trap that caught the British General Charles Cornwallis at Yorktown, Virginia, and effectively ended the Revolutionary War.

Unfortunately, the sort of recklessness that brought Henry Lee success on the battlefield led to downfall in his personal life. After resigning his command in 1782, Lee married his cousin Matilda. He then invested much of his wife's considerable tobacco fortune, as well as money from friends, in rash real estate schemes. Carried away by dreams of wealth, Lee plotted the founding of magnificent new cities in western lands, particularly Mississippi. Henry lost so much money in these investments that Matilda grew fearful that there would be nothing left to pass on as an inheritance to her children. When Matilda died suddenly in 1790, her will stated that most of her remaining wealth was to be given not to Henry but to her children.

Still a popular figure in Virginia, Henry was elected governor of that state in 1791. He then courted Ann Carter, the 20-year-old daughter of Charles Carter, one of the richest men in Virginia. Ann was flattered by the attention of such a prominent man, but her father had his suspicions. Mr. Carter refused to allow the marriage unless Lee gave up his latest wild adventure—a plan to join the armies of the French Revolution. The 37-year-old Lee agreed to stay at home, and he married Ann in 1793.

Light Horse Harry had one last moment of glory in 1794. President Washington called upon Lee to lead 15,000 soldiers against a group of farmers in Pennsylvania who were rebelling against a new whiskey tax. The uprising was easily crushed, and the affair added more prestige to Henry's name. Some talked of him as a successor to President Washington. In fact, Lee was so closely linked with the president that he was asked to deliver the eulogy at Washington's funeral in 1799. Lee paid Washington a tribute that has lasted through the ages: "First in war, first in peace, and first in the hearts of his countrymen." Lee's political ambitions ended, however, when his Federalist Party was swept from power in 1800 by Thomas Jefferson and the Democratic-Republicans.

"Light Horse Harry" was a colonial hero.

During his political career, Henry Lee held on to his dreams of riches in the West. He poured his new wife's money after the lost money of his former wife, traveling far from home to arrange real estate deals. The results were disastrous. By the time Robert Edward was born on January 19, 1807,

George Washington counted Henry Lee among his closest associates.

the Lees' home, the once-magnificent Stratford Hall in Westmoreland County, Virginia, was in shambles. The rooms were cold and bare. Most of the furniture had been sold off to pay debts. One entire wing of the house was abandoned.

In Robert's early years, his father was constantly dodging creditors. The entrances to the house were chained to keep the sheriff from seizing more property to pay Henry Lee's debts. Rather than learning from his financial mistakes, Henry bet everything on one last real estate scheme. He lost $40,000 and was sent to debtors' prison.

In a further humiliation to the family, Henry's only surviving son from his first marriage, Henry, Jr., decided to claim his inheritance. In 1811, he took over Stratford Hall, which had once belonged to his mother, Matilda. His father's family was forced to move out. They settled in Alexandria, Virginia, and lived on money from a trust account left to Ann by her father. The money provided for basic food, shelter, and clothing, but nothing else.

Henry Lee was out of prison, but he was a broken man. He was haunted by shame about his irresponsible dealings. A vicious beating in Baltimore in 1812 provided the final humiliation. Attacked for opposing war with Great Britain, Light Horse Harry was badly beaten by a drunken mob. With all his money, pride, health, and hope gone, Lee sailed for the Caribbean islands. Six years later, he attempted to return, but he died on the Georgia coast without ever seeing his family again.

Robert, who was six when his father left, was forced to grow up in a hurry. Robert's two older brothers, Carter and Smith, left home and busied themselves with their careers. Meanwhile, Ann Lee's health began to collapse; eventually she was restricted to a wheelchair. Robert's older sister, Ann, was also in poor health, so it was left to Robert to run the household, which included a younger sister, Mildred. By the time he was 13, Robert was doing the shopping and the housekeeping, keeping up the grounds, rationing out his mother's medicine, and carrying her to her carriage when she needed to travel.

Robert enjoyed swimming and playing sports with his cousins in Alexandria. But his responsibilities left him little leisure time. Robert's mother drilled him on the importance of those qualities that had been so lacking in his father: self-denial, patience, and responsibility. There was the further bad example of Robert's spendthrift brother, Carter, who was squandering meager family funds by living a party life at Harvard College.

Robert's responsible behavior won him the respect of neighbors, friends, and especially his mother. "How can I live without Robert?" his mother once said. "He is son, daughter and everything to me!" He was rewarded with boundless love and appreciation and gained deep satisfaction from easing his mother's pain. Despite the rigorous demands placed on him, Robert remained cheerful.

Although his family had little money and no land, Robert was still a Lee, and his mother was still a Carter. They were related by blood and marriage to many of Virginia's wealthiest and most influential landowners and politicians. They were descendants of some of colonial America's greatest statesmen. As such, the Lees were entitled to some of the privileges that went with their respected name. The Carters had set up both a boys' school and a girls' school for the private instruction of their children. Robert spent two years at school with his cousins before enrolling in the Alexandria Academy in 1820. After three years of excellent work at this preparatory school, it was time for the 17-year-old to think about his career.

Despite his excellent marks at school, Lee found few options available to him. He did not have land to farm, nor did his family have money to provide him with a college education. Lee's best chance seemed to be to follow in the footsteps of his father in the military. The tuition at the United States Military Academy at West Point, New York, would be paid by the government—if Robert could win an appointment. Competition for the 250 openings at West Point was stiff, but Robert could count on the influence of his Lee and Carter relatives, as well as his own outstanding academic record. Robert was accepted at West Point and entered the Academy in 1825.

In the end, however, the name of Lee was to be more of a curse than a blessing. Robert had to live down not only the shameful behavior of his father but also that of his half-brother, Henry, Jr. After a sordid affair with his wife's younger sister, Henry Lee, Jr., had been dubbed "Black Horse Harry." The scandal was the subject of rumors for several years, and the newspapers covered it extensively when it came to light in 1830. Henry Lee, Jr., had fled out West in disgrace. The episode so tarnished the family name that Robert held little hope that any respectable woman would marry him.

At West Point, Robert continued the nearly perfect behavior that contrasted strongly with the embarrassments of his relatives. He devoted himself to his studies and ranked near the top of his class throughout his years at the Academy. He did not drink or swear. He was impeccably neat, clean, and well mannered, and he received no demerits for violating any of the Army's most picky rules. Lee's spotless behavior led some classmates to call him "the Marble

Model." But Lee was not one to criticize other cadets for their behavior. He was well liked and faced none of the resentment, jealousy, or ridicule that perfect behavior often breeds among classmates.

Lee's remarkable record seems to have resulted more from his self-discipline than from a natural gift for learning. Lee far preferred active, outdoor activities such as horseback riding to studying. His gracious manner and friendly nature made him a popular party guest. But he read far more than was required for his coursework. By his fourth year, Robert was named adjutant of the corps of cadets—the Academy's highest-ranking student.

The hardest Academy rule for Robert to endure was the one stating that no cadet could leave the Academy for the first two years. Robert hated to be separated from his mother, whose health continued to slip. Upon graduating with honors in 1829, Lee rushed home to be with his mother, who was by this time desperately ill. Ann Lee could find no comfort except in the company of her son. Robert was constantly at her bedside. After one month, she died.

THREE

The Engineer
1829-1849

Robert, with no more family ties to restrict him, accepted his first military assignment at Cockspur Island near Savannah, Georgia. As a top student at West Point, he had earned membership in the elite Army Corps of Engineers. But it was a mixed blessing. On Cockspur Island, Lee's tasks consisted mainly of routine construction work that involved shoring up run-down Army forts.

The work on Cockspur Island, which sits in an isolated, mosquito-infested portion of the Savannah River, was particularly dreary. Lee often slogged through knee-high mud as he supervised the construction work.

Those who knew him described the black-haired, brown-eyed Lee as one of the most handsome men in Virginia. He stood 5 feet, 11 inches (180 centimeters) tall and carried himself with confidence. This, added to his charming manner, strong character, and admirable work habits, should have made Lee one of society's most sought-after bachelors. But

Mary Custis Lee had illustrious bloodlines. Her great-grandmother was Martha Washington (left).

the Black Horse Harry scandal had hit the press just after Robert's graduation. The scandal, Robert's lack of wealth, and his father's unfortunate legacy combined to make Lee suspect.

Robert courted a cousin whom he had known since childhood, Mary Anna Randolph Custis. Mary's father was the grandson of Martha Washington and the adopted son of George Washington. Along with illustrious ancestry, Mary held title to a good deal of wealth. As the only one of the four Custis children to survive early childhood, she stood to inherit two large estates near Washington, D.C., and more than 200 slaves. Robert and Mary were married in June of 1831. Robert had been transferred to Fort Monroe in Virginia a month before. Mary's father was not convinced that Robert was good enough for his daughter, but he agreed to allow the marriage.

Mary seemed particularly unsuited to military life. When she joined Robert at his new post at Fort Monroe, she was easily bored, disliked socializing with other military wives at the parties where her husband was in great demand, and fretted about Robert's imposed limit of two personal slaves. After a short time, Mary persuaded Robert to let her go home to her family estate at Arlington, Virginia, for a visit. The "visit" stretched into months. In September 1832, the Lees' first child was born at Arlington. From that time on, separation was more the rule than the exception for the couple. Mary and Robert eventually had seven children: Custis, Mary, William (nicknamed Rooney), Agnes, Annie, Robert, Jr., and Mildred. Each time Mary became pregnant, she returned to live among the Custis clan at Arlington.

Lee's professional life was far from satisfying in those early years of marriage. His work at Fort Monroe, directing construction projects, was repeatedly marred by disputes between engineers and soldiers. For a while, the highly trained Lee was doing nothing more than supervising men who were piling stones for foundations.

In 1834 Lee was so eager for fresh tasks that, even though he hated the thought of working at a desk job, he accepted a new position in the Army's Chief of Engineers Office in Washington, D.C. The work proved to be as tedious as he had feared. Lee broke from the routine in 1835 when he

Lee's military career frequently took him far from his wife, Mary, and his home at Arlington.

went west to help settle a border dispute between Ohio and Michigan. While Lee was away, his wife delivered her second child. After the delivery, Mary became very sick and was bedridden for months. When Lee returned home, he found his wife in severe pain. Although Mary recovered from this bout with illness, she was never fully healthy again. Eventually, Lee was forced to tend to a bedridden wife, just as he had taken care of his invalid mother.

Lee's military assignments continued to take him away from home. The frequent separations bothered Lee, who wished to spend more time with his growing family. Haunted by the memory of his own father, he worried about the effect his absences would have on his children. Robert tried to make up for his absences by sending his children long letters.

As a father Robert found himself pulled in different directions by his various duties. When eight-year-old Rooney accidentally sliced the tips of his fingers with a straw cutter, Robert Lee the disciplinarian felt compelled to lecture the boy about safety. Yet Robert Lee the loving father would sit at his children's bedsides for nights on end to see them through various childhood illnesses.

Lee could be a most patient and forgiving teacher. But he was a perfectionist. He would map out in intricate detail the steps his children would have to follow in learning to swim or ride horseback. He expected equally detailed reports from them on their progress.

As a military officer, Lee willingly undertook whatever hardship was assigned to him. But he was sometimes paralyzed with indecision when one duty conflicted with another. For most of his career, he agonized over whether he should continue to carry out the military tasks for which he was trained or whether he should resign so that he could spend time with his family. Frequently he expressed a wish to settle down with his family and find some land to farm. "In all my schemes of happiness I look forward to returning to some quiet corner among the hills of Virginia," he said.

The once-vivacious party-goer slipped into periods of deep depression and began to wonder if he was wasting his time in a military career. "I am waiting, looking and hoping for some good opportunity to bid an affectionate farewell to my dear Uncle Sam," he wrote to a former commanding officer in 1835.

Lee's military duties offered few perks to make up for the loss of his family life. Army pay was meager, and advancement through the ranks came slowly. Shamed by memories of his father's behavior, Lee hated to dip into his wife's money to provide wanted comforts.

Following his wife's recovery in 1836, Lee happily accepted an assignment in St. Louis, Missouri—hoping to escape the routine engineering work at home.

In St. Louis, Lee was assigned a difficult task—finding a way to prevent the shifting sand bars in the Mississippi River from blocking the city's harbor. Mary and the children joined him there in 1838, but when Mary became pregnant, she again headed back to Virginia to stay with her family at Arlington.

Robert's success in rerouting the river channel received great praise, and Lee was promoted to captain. Unfortunately, the federal government was short of money and could create no desirable assignment with which to reward him. Taking the best of some poor choices, Lee accepted the job of repairing a series of forts and batteries in New York Harbor. Again, he brought his family to stay with him. Again, Mary left for home when she became pregnant.

The task of fortifying and updating the New York facilities was a massive, time-consuming effort. Lee kept at it for five years. In 1846, when hostilities began to brew between the United States and Mexico, the 39-year-old Lee was still a low-ranking officer doing mundane chores for the peacetime Army.

FOUR

The Best Soldier in Christendom

1846-1848

Robert E. Lee was not proud when the United States, hoping to win vast amounts of disputed territory in the American Southwest, declared war on Mexico in 1846. "We have bullied her [Mexico]. For that I am ashamed," he said. It seemed to Lee that the United States had provoked a fight with its southern neighbor. The affair bolstered Lee's lifelong dislike of politics. But once war had been declared, Lee never wavered in his determination to carry out his duties to the best of his ability.

His role in the Mexican conflict began with a typically routine assignment—the construction of roads and bridges in Texas and New Mexico. In January 1847, General Winfield Scott, the leader of the United States forces opposing Mexico, selected Lee to join his personal staff for the Mexican invasion. Lee proved to be particularly skilled at scouting out terrain, discovering the enemy's defensive weaknesses, and putting artillery in the most advantageous positions.

It was dangerous work. Returning to camp before the attack on Veracruz, Mexico, Lee was accidentally fired on by a United States sentry. The bullet passed between Lee's left arm and his chest, singeing his uniform. Lee was unruffled by the encounter and proceeded with his assignment. He successfully positioned six enormous cannon within 700 yards (640 meters) of Veracruz without the enemy spotting them.

On another occasion, Lee climbed into the mountains near Cerro Gordo on a scouting mission. While checking out a mountain pass to see if it would be possible to build a road through it, he heard men speaking Spanish. With no escape route available, Lee hid under a large log.

Unfortunately, Lee happened to have stumbled upon a spring that Mexican troops were using for water. As soon as one group of Mexican soldiers left, another would arrive. Many of the soldiers sat on the very log under which Lee was hiding! Lee lay motionless for hours until nightfall. Finally the Mexicans left, and Lee had to make his way down the treacherous ravine in the dark.

The Cerro Gordo campaign gave Lee a chance to display his intelligence as well as his courage. The Mexican army had been keeping to the high mountain passes, areas that seemed inaccessible to the heavy American artillery. Lee's job was to find a way to haul the heavy guns into the mountains. At the same time he was to direct a column of soldiers in the battle that would follow. Lee scouted out a route, moved the guns into position with ropes and pulleys, and then stationed his brigade in the Mexican army's path of retreat. Lee performed his duties so well that the U.S. forces captured 3,000 Mexican soldiers and most of their artillery.

As the invasion moved on to Mexico City, Lee again performed with courage and cunning. The United States

Army had boldly struck out toward the capital city in the interior of Mexico without setting up a line of supplies from the coast. That meant that unless they captured the well-guarded city, and did so quickly, the entire U.S. Army was likely to be destroyed.

Mexico City posed a baffling problem for an invading army. Its defenses were strong on all sides. The roads leading from the south were lined with strong patrols, and the only other approach to the city was through a baked wilderness of lava stones known as the *pedregal*. This scorched, rugged terrain was considered impassable, especially for a large army with heavy equipment.

Undaunted, Lee scouted out a route and pushed into the barren wilderness with a group of soldiers. Lee lost communication with the main army when Scott's messengers failed to find their way through the lava field. So Lee returned to find Scott himself. Moving through the pedregal by daylight

A newspaper illustration of the day shows General Scott's troops storming a Mexican fortress.

was difficult enough, but attempting to cross at night was nearly suicidal. Deep fissures cut sharply through the lava beds; an unsuspecting soldier could easily plunge to his death.

Seven scouts sent from Scott's army to the southeast of the pedregal had turned back without finding Lee's party. Yet within 36 hours, without a moment's sleep, Lee made three trips through the grueling terrain to report his position and rejoin Scott's troops.

Because of Lee's astounding maneuvers, Scott's army caught the defenders off guard and made easy work of the approach. Once in range of Mexico City, Lee put in 48 more hours of continuous work constructing artillery platforms. The effort paid off. Scott's army captured the Mexican capital. Mexico was defeated, and the United States gained huge tracts of land in the American Southwest.

Even a veteran commander such as General Scott had never in his career witnessed a single soldier accomplish so much. At the war's end, Scott groped to find adequate words to express his admiration. If anyone was to take credit for the success of the daring expedition to Mexico City, said Scott, it would have to be Robert E. Lee. Lee, he said, was "the best soldier in Christendom." Upon entering Mexico City, Scott offered a toast to Lee, the man "without whose aid we should not now be here."

Such lavish praise in the high reaches of the armed forces might have propelled Lee swiftly up the military ranks at last. But with the end of the war, the Army once again had little to do but take up tedious fort-building projects. There was little turnover among the high-ranking Army officers. When promotions were available, they were frequently handed out as political favors. Lee, who detested this system of favoritism, was bypassed, while officers with a fraction of his credentials were rewarded.

Slavery was legal in the early United States. But many people, particularly Northerners, opposed the practice and sought to wipe it out across the entire nation.

FIVE

The Growing Storm

1848-1860

After rejoining his family for a brief time following the Mexican conflict, Lee moved on to Baltimore to begin another series of routine fortification assignments. It was as if his heroics in Mexico had never taken place. Lee was still floundering in the low ranks of the Army, enduring long stretches of separation from his family.

Some of the monotony was broken when Lee was appointed superintendent of the U.S. Military Academy. The assignment was meant as an honor, but Lee tried to avoid it, claiming he lacked the necessary experience to lead the Academy. The Army, however, ignored his protests, and Lee agreed to take the position in 1852.

The experience was valuable in many ways. For the first time in years, Lee's military living quarters were suitable for his family, and Mary and the children came to live with him at West Point. In his new position, Lee gained insight into methods of dealing with young soldiers. He was also able to make the acquaintance of fine young cadets such as James E. B. "Jeb" Stuart and powerful statesmen such as Secretary of War Jefferson Davis. Both friendships would prove valuable in later years.

As Lee settled into his new position, his religious convictions grew stronger. Lee was confirmed in 1853. Before then, he had not belonged to a church. But as he grew older, his actions came to be guided more and more by his spiritual beliefs.

Despite the advantages of life at West Point, Lee was never comfortable as superintendent. Kind and conscientious, Lee worried about the progress of each cadet. He disliked having to discipline the high-spirited youngsters and kept close tabs on those who were struggling with their school work.

As much as he loved being able to spend time with his family, Lee felt he had no choice but to accept a rare opportunity for advancement in 1855. At the age of 48, Lee was promoted to lieutenant colonel and was made second-in-command of a new cavalry unit formed in the state of Texas.

Lee reported to Camp Cooper, Texas, in March 1855. But the assignment was hardly a prize one. Lee's work on the Texas frontier—protecting military outposts from Mexican and Comanche raiders—was hot, gritty, and frustrating. On top of that, Lee frequently had to ride long distances to sit in judgment on court martial cases, a role he disliked. It was not long before he fell back into loneliness and depression.

In late 1856, Lee received word that Mary's father, George Washington Custis, had died. He requested a leave of absence to help settle his father-in-law's affairs. Upon reaching Virginia in November, Lee found his wife crippled with arthritis and confined to a wheelchair.

Mr. Custis's Arlington estate was losing money and was badly in need of repair. Yet the prospects for repairing the property were poor. Mr. Custis's will provided for his slaves to be given their freedom over a period of years, so labor would be in short supply. Upon closer inspection, the task of settling the Custis property proved more exhausting than anyone had expected. A tangled web of hidden debts and complicated financial deals needed to be put in order. Although not convinced he had the business expertise required for the job, Lee worked diligently to organize the documents. The task was overwhelming. When Robert's leave from the Army expired, he applied for several extensions to complete the job.

Lee's daughter Agnes

Lee had been home struggling with the Custis estate for over two years when he was called back for military service. A Kansas farmer, John Brown, struck a blow that widened the growing rift between Northern abolitionists (those opposed to slavery) and Southern slave owners.

The practice of slavery, which had been legal since the country's founding, was concentrated in the South. The Southern states depended more heavily on agriculture than did the industrial North. Many Southern growers profited by using black slaves as agricultural laborers, and most opposed any disruption to this system.

But by the early 1800s, an abolition movement had begun in the North. The abolitionists believed slavery was immoral, and they sought to end it throughout the United States. The movement gained momentum in the North but aroused bitter opposition in the South. Congress passed several laws in the 1850s hoping to bring about compromises between the pro- and antislavery forces. But the tension continued to build. Many Southern leaders believed that each state government had the right to decide for itself whether or not to allow slavery, and they resented interference from the North.

John Brown believed passionately that slavery was a hideous evil and that his mission in life was to end it. Brown would stop at nothing, not even murder, in his efforts to abolish slavery. In 1859, Brown and a band of his followers traveled east with dreams of liberating the slaves. Their plan was to capture a supply of weapons and ammunition at a government armory in Harpers Ferry, on Virginia's northern border. They would then march through the South distributing these arms to slaves, who would join them in a massive uprising against the slave owners.

Black slaves worked as laborers, field hands, and household servants. Some Southerners thought their businesses and farms could not prosper without slave labor.

Brown accomplished the first part of his plan, the seizing of the armory, on October 17. The federal government took immediate action to stop him. There was no time to wait for a high-ranking Army officer to travel to Harpers Ferry. Army personnel scanned the roster to see if there was a capable officer in the immediate area. They came up with the name of a Mexican War hero, a lieutenant colonel on leave from his command in Texas—Robert E. Lee.

Lieutenant Jeb Stuart galloped down from Washington with orders for Lee to report to Harpers Ferry. There Lee was to take command of a collection of state militia and United States Marines. Lee arrived at the armory on the evening of October 17 and quickly sized up the situation.

Many people hoped to resolve the debate over slavery in a peaceful manner. John Brown, however, supported a violent slave uprising.

Brown and his followers, several already killed or wounded by state militia, were now inside one of the armory buildings with several hostages. State and federal troops surrounded the building and waited through the night. When Brown refused to surrender, Lee ordered the storming of the armory. John Brown and 12 of his followers were quickly captured. One soldier and another of Brown's men were killed in the process.

In February Lee returned to his command in Texas. The bitter dispute between the states disturbed him deeply. Although he had owned slaves as a result of marriage into the Custis family, Lee opposed the institution. "In this enlightened age, there are few I believe, but what will acknowledge, that slavery as an institution, is a moral and political evil in any Country," he wrote to his wife.

As the slavery issue became more heated, there was growing sentiment among Southern politicians that they should secede from the United States and form their own country. Lee strongly opposed such an idea. "I wish to live under no other government, and there is no sacrifice I am not ready to make for the preservation of the Union [the United States] save that of honour," he said. As a lifelong admirer of George Washington and the other colonial leaders, Lee was appalled that their magnificent efforts to form a unified nation might go to waste.

At the same time, Lee was loyal to his native state. The Lees had been proud Virginians since colonial days, long before the United States was an independent nation. As a descendent of the Virginia elite, Robert believed firmly in the right of states to govern themselves without interference from the central government. He thought that slavery should be and would be phased out by the Southern states themselves. He believed that Northern abolitionists had no business trying to dictate policy to the entire nation.

As he resumed his duties in the dry heat of the Texas plains in February 1860, Lee hoped that people in both sections of the country would not get carried away by their passions. Some radicals were calling excitedly for a war between the North and South. In Mexico, Lee had seen firsthand the hideous nature of war. He had written to his son Custis at the time: "You have no idea what a horrible sight a field of battle is."

But it was already too late to head off the growing storm. In December 1860, South Carolina reacted to the election of President Abraham Lincoln, an antislavery Republican, by seceding from the Union. Other Southern states quickly followed. As the Southerners were organizing a new government, the Confederate States of America, the federal government made it clear that it would use force, if necessary, to bring the "Rebels" back into the Union. War was coming.

Immediately after his election, Abraham Lincoln became the leader of a divided nation.

SIX

The Call of Duty

1861-1862

On February 1, 1861, the state of Texas voted to secede from the United States and join the Confederate States of America. This put Lee, who was by then in command of his own cavalry unit, in an awkward and dangerous position. He was in charge of a U.S. Army regiment that was suddenly in the middle of enemy territory, surrounded by hostile citizens. Other Army officers in Texas, sympathetic to the Southern cause, had handed over their equipment to the new Confederate nation. Lee found the idea appalling. How could someone who had sworn faithful service to the United States of America suddenly surrender all of his government property to a band of rebels? It disturbed him greatly to see American flags being yanked down and replaced with Texas and Confederate flags.

Lee escaped his precarious situation in Texas when, on February 13, he was ordered to report to Washington, D.C. But his dilemma only grew worse. Federal officials hoped that Lee would remain loyal to the Union. On March 28, Lee was offered a promotion to full colonel, which he accepted.

Then, General Winfield Scott offered Lee the chance of a lifetime. Aging and overweight, General Scott could no longer command a force on the battlefield. Most of the experienced, high-ranking officers in the United States Army were Southerners who were resigning to join the Confederate cause. Remembering Lee's exploits in Mexico, Scott asked if Lee would take command of a federal army. On April 18, Lee received a formal offer from President Lincoln: Would Lee take field command of a Union army that could number upwards of 100,000 men?

For a 54-year-old man who had labored without much reward for so long, it was a dream come true. After all the doubts, monotony, and loneliness, here was proof at last that Lee's efforts had not been wasted.

But Lee wavered. Again, his sense of duty gave him conflicting signals. On one hand, he felt bound by his oath of loyalty to the United States. He wanted to see the Union preserved. Accepting the command would also be a wise career move and would offer him a good means of providing for his family.

On the other hand, Lee was disturbed by the thought of leading an invasion against his neighboring states in the South. There was also the question of what Virginia would do. Lee had declared earlier that, if war came, his first loyalty would be to his native Virginia. Although Virginia had recently voted against secession by a two-to-one margin, it was plain that the state's sympathies rested with the South.

When General Scott could not persuade Lee to accept command of the Union forces, he sadly commented, "Lee, you have made the greatest mistake of your life, but I feared it would be so." A Virginian himself, Scott was neither

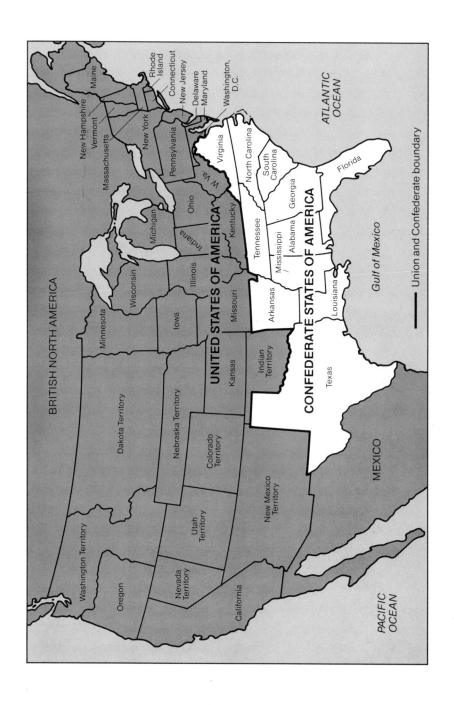

ATLANTIC OCEAN

Union and Confederate boundary

BRITISH NORTH AMERICA

UNITED STATES OF AMERICA

CONFEDERATE STATES OF AMERICA

Maine

New Hampshire
Vermont
Massachusetts
Rhode Island
Connecticut
New York
New Jersey
Delaware
Maryland
Washington, D.C.
Pennsylvania
W. Va.
Virginia
North Carolina
South Carolina

Ohio
Michigan
Indiana
Kentucky
Tennessee
Georgia
Alabama
Mississippi
Florida

Wisconsin
Illinois
Missouri
Arkansas
Louisiana

Minnesota
Iowa
Kansas
Indian Territory
Texas

Dakota Territory
Nebraska Territory
Colorado Territory
New Mexico Territory

Washington Territory
Oregon
Nevada Territory
Utah Territory
California

Gulf of Mexico

MEXICO

PACIFIC OCEAN

As a loyal U.S. Army officer, Lee was greatly distressed by Southern secession.

surprised nor angered by Lee's decision. He suggested that Lee ought to resign from the Army.

Although this was just what Lee had been considering for many years, it was nonetheless a difficult decision. The very day after Lee declined Lincoln's offer, he received the somber news that Virginia had reversed its decision and was severing its ties with the United States. That night, Lee wrote a letter to the United States secretary of war, Simon Cameron:

Sir:

I have the honor to tender the resignation of my commission as Colonel of the 1st Regt. of Cavalry.

Very resp'y Your Obedient Servant.

R.E. Lee

Col 1st Cav'ry

Lee's professional evaluation of the growing hostilities told him that the outlook would be grim for the South. "The war may last ten years," he wrote to his wife. He foresaw a long and brutal conflict, in which the Northern states would hold the overwhelming advantage. They were far wealthier, produced more than 95 percent of the nation's firearms, commanded a far stronger navy, and outnumbered Southerners, 22 million to 9 million. Lee was also aware that if he sided with the Rebels, it would be impossible for him to defend his home in Arlington against the Union forces concentrated directly across the Potomac River in Washington, D.C.

Although Lee did not try to influence his sons' decisions regarding the conflict, all three chose to serve the Confederacy. Despite his mixed feelings, Lee's sense of duty would not let him sit out of the approaching conflict himself.

Many Southerners were eager to fight and quickly organized Confederate regiments.

When the government of Virginia asked him to assume command of the state's military forces, Lee felt bound by duty to accept. Regardless of his expectations for success, Lee believed it was the right thing to do. As for the outcome of the war, he said, "God knows what is best for us." The only regret Lee expressed in accepting command was the modest wish that the state could have found an abler man to do the job.

Lee immediately set about preparing a defense for the Northern attack that was soon to come. Virginia, the northernmost of the Confederate states, bordered the Union capital of Washington, D.C. Virginia would be directly in the path of any advance by Northern troops. Feelings ran so strong in the dispute between the states that many Southern soldiers were eager to fight. But Lee realized that the battles to come would more likely be won by organization and preparation than by strength and courage. It was Lee's task to develop an efficient means of moving, supplying, and positioning troops.

He selected a site near Manassas Junction, Virginia, 25 miles (40 kilometers) southwest of Washington, to make a stand against the expected invasion. At the same time, he concentrated a small force at Harpers Ferry under the command of a Virginia Military Institute professor named Thomas Jackson, and he strengthened the defenses at the naval yards in Norfolk, Virginia.

The task of securing able Confederate officers was complicated by political confusion. At the same time that the Virginia militia was organizing independently, the Confederate States of America was putting together its national army. Lee attempted to recruit an old friend, Joseph Johnston, to help him coordinate the Virginia defense. Johnston, however, chose to accept a position in the Confederate army instead.

Confederate generals Pierre Beauregard (above) *and Joseph Johnston* (left) *took command in Virginia.*

The confusion continued when, several weeks later, the Virginia forces were transferred to the command of the Confederacy. Lee was commissioned as one of the Confederate army's highest ranking generals, but by that time the assignments had already been made. Generals Johnston and Pierre Beauregard took over command of the armies defending Virginia (which at that time included the present-day states of Virginia and West Virginia), while Lee was virtually left out of the picture.

The newly chosen Confederate president, Jefferson Davis, had developed a high regard for Robert E. Lee during Lee's stint as West Point supervisor. Davis wanted to keep Lee close at hand as an advisor. As a result, Lee was far from the battlefield when the first major clash of the war took place along Bull Run Creek at Manassas, Virginia.

The Confederates scored a stunning victory over the advancing Union troops at Bull Run, prompting Southerners to praise Johnston and Beauregard as heroes. Lee, who had set the stage for victory, was ignored.

In the fall of 1861, Lee was dispatched to western Virginia on a difficult assignment. Three small Confederate armies had taken a severe battering in that mountainous region. Lee was supposed to help them regroup and halt the advancing Union army.

Confederate president
Jefferson Davis

It proved to be an impossible situation. Many of the residents of the area were pro-Union and offered support to the federal troops. Lee's forces had no reliable maps to guide them through the twisting ravines and mountain passes and no scouting service to provide them with information about the enemy. Heavy rains, muddy roads, and sickness thwarted their progress. The leaders of the Confederate units seemed more intent on quarreling with each other than on fighting the enemy. Instead of taking charge of the situation, Lee tried to play peacemaker among the feuding factions. His low-key approach to this infighting did not work and prompted criticism that he was "too tender of blood" to lead an army.

Despite the setbacks, Lee carefully positioned the troops for an assault against the more numerous Union forces. Just as the attack was to get under way, however, one of Lee's flank commanders decided that the enemy held a stronger position than he had expected. The officer refused to send his soldiers into action, and the attack had to be called off. It was the only opportunity Lee would get to push the Federals from the area. Within a few weeks, he abandoned his failed campaign and withdrew from the region. This mountainous area was newly designated as the state of West Virginia, and it stayed pro-Union throughout the war.

General Lee's only accomplishment during the campaign had been the growing of a silvery beard. He had managed to lose a large section of Virginia without firing a shot in defense. Confederate leaders dubbed him "Granny Lee" for his timidity. It also cast doubt on Lee's dedication to the Confederate cause. After all, it was no secret that Lee had opposed secession. During the first days of the rebellion, when many Southerners had boasted loudly of their ability to whip the "Yankees"—as they called the Northerners—Lee had been almost gloomy. He quietly cautioned that it would be a long struggle and that the South should prepare to suffer. All of this caused some Confederate officials to wonder whether Lee's heart was really in his work. When Lee was transferred to South Carolina after the debacle in western Virginia, South Carolinian officials protested heatedly.

Lee's second assignment was to build up coastal defenses to protect South Carolina and Georgia from naval attack. This job proved somewhat easier, but no more noteworthy, than Lee's first assignment. When Jefferson Davis summoned him back to the Confederate capital of Richmond, Virginia, in March 1862, Lee still had done nothing to win the trust, or even the notice, of many Southerners.

Richmond now faced a deadly threat from the North. After many months of training, Union General George McClellan had finally begun marching toward Richmond with his mighty Army of the Potomac. With more than 100,000

Union and Confederate army barracks were usually crude huts that provided little protection or comfort to the soldiers.

blue-coated troops under his command, McClellan chose to attack Richmond from the peninsula to the east of the city. At the same time, another powerful Union force under General Irvin McDowell was sweeping down from the North.

Opposing McClellan were about 70,000 Confederates in the Richmond area, led by Joe Johnston. Another 25,000 Confederate soldiers shadowed McDowell to the north. Yet there seemed to be little the Confederates could do to avoid being caught in a vise between the two Union armies. If McDowell joined McClellan near Richmond, that city would be lost. Somehow, the Confederates had to stop McDowell.

Upon Lee's advice, General Thomas Jackson (nicknamed Stonewall because his brigade stood "like a stone wall" at Bull Run) attacked the Union forces that were defending Washington. Jackson's success caused the United States government to worry about the safety of its capital city. Accordingly, McDowell's army, which had come within 25 miles (40 km) of McClellan, was ordered back to defend the capital. McDowell's threat, for the time being, was removed.

But there was still the matter of McClellan's huge army approaching Richmond from the peninsula. On June 1, 1862, Johnston's army fought desperately to keep McClellan's heavy artillery from advancing within range of the Confederate capital. During a series of attacks and counterattacks, General Johnston was wounded and carried from the field. Jefferson Davis selected Lee, who had been growing restless waiting for another assignment, to take command of Johnston's army.

SEVEN

The Army of Northern Virginia

1862-1863

Lee inherited a difficult situation because Johnston had kept his battle plans secret. But the new commander realized that McClellan not only outnumbered him in troops but also enjoyed a huge advantage in artillery. McClellan's strategy of advancing slowly under the protection of well-entrenched artillery left Lee in a terrible position. It would be suicidal for him to attack McClellan in the face of such firepower. Yet if he did not attack, McClellan would grind his way so close to Richmond that he could level it with his artillery. Lee had to figure out a way to lure the Army of the Potomac away from its strong position.

Lee was acquainted with McClellan from their days in the Mexican War when both had served on the staff of Winfield Scott. "He is an able general, but a very cautious one," Lee explained to one of his generals. The best strategies for attacking such a man, in Lee's view, were surprise and intimidation.

Few of Lee's own soldiers thought him capable of accomplishing either. While many officers were aware of Lee's ability, the average Southern soldier knew little about him. When he immediately ordered his men to dig trenches and build defensive works out of earth and timber, it seemed like more of Granny Lee's timid strategy. Some soldiers gave him another insulting nickname: "King of Spades." Little did they know that the construction work was all part of a surprise that Lee had arranged for McClellan. While the trenches were being dug, Lee sent a detachment of cavalry, led by General Jeb Stuart, on a dashing ride around McClellan's army.

Stuart discovered a weakness in the right flank of the Union lines. But some Confederate generals wondered if Lee was bold enough to exploit this advantage. Colonel Joseph Ives, remembering Lee's courageous feats in Mexico, eased their fears. "If there is any man in either army head and shoulders above every other in audacity, it is General Lee!" Ives said. "He will take more desperate chances and take them quicker than any other general in this country. . . ."

One basic rule of military strategy states that a general should never divide an army in the presence of a superior force. Lee predicted that a responsible, cautious general such as McClellan would not dream that his enemy would violate the rule. But that was just what Lee proposed to do. Contrary to appearances, Lee was not digging his army into a defensive shell. The massive earthworks he had erected would only help protect a thin line of troops that he would leave to guard the entrance to Richmond. Lee would then shift the rest of his army to the west. Stonewall Jackson's divisions would march down from the north and join him. Together they would overwhelm the Army of the Potomac's right flank and encircle the bulk of McClellan's force.

George McClellan had a huge army at his command. But he failed to press his advantage against Lee.

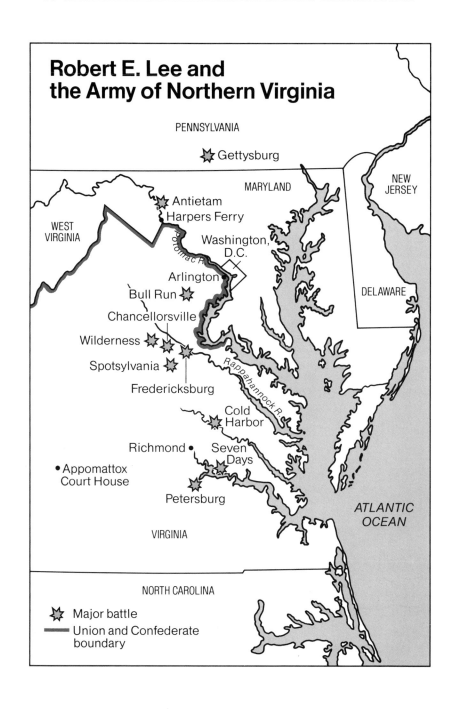

Robert E. Lee and the Army of Northern Virginia

PENNSYLVANIA

⭐ Gettysburg

MARYLAND

NEW JERSEY

WEST VIRGINIA

⭐ Antietam
Harpers Ferry

Washington, D.C.

Potomac R.

Arlington

Bull Run ⭐

DELAWARE

Chancellorsville

Wilderness ⭐

Spotsylvania ⭐

Fredericksburg

Rappahannock R.

Cold Harbor ⭐

Richmond ●

Seven Days ⭐

● Appomattox Court House

Petersburg ⭐

VIRGINIA

ATLANTIC OCEAN

NORTH CAROLINA

⭐ Major battle

━━━ Union and Confederate boundary

The dangers were extraordinary. If the Yankees realized that there were only 25,000 Confederate soldiers defending Richmond, they would easily smash through and capture the city. But Lee believed he could prevent McClellan from attempting such a strike.

McClellan's cautious nature frequently led him to overestimate the strength of the enemy. Faulty scouting reports led him to believe that the Confederates defending Richmond actually outnumbered him. Lee encouraged this delusion by having several of his companies mill about in open view. Then, leaving a thin screen of soldiers behind, those same companies would move farther down the line and parade again in front of the Yankee scouts. Confederate artillery corps erected "Quaker guns"—large logs sticking out of earthworks that from a distance appeared to be cannon. Union scouts dutifully counted heads and guns and came up with wildly inaccurate estimates of the enemy's strength. At one point McClellan believed the Confederates outnumbered the Federals two to one, and he pleaded for reinforcements. McClellan was more cautious than ever.

When Lee hurled a furious assault at the Yankee right flank, McClellan did not suspect that this was actually the bulk of the Rebel force. The attack pushed the Federals back toward the peninsula. Had Lee's intricate plan been carried out perfectly, McClellan's huge army might have been destroyed.

Unfortunately, Lee was demanding a degree of precision that his lieutenants could not produce. For one of the few times in his career, Stonewall Jackson failed to carry out his assignment. Not only was he late in arriving with his soldiers, he was also strangely indecisive in bringing support to Lee's attacking troops. To make matters worse, General James "Pete" Longstreet had taken the wrong road and was late in reaching his destination. Mistakes such as these helped the Union troops slow down the Confederate charge. The Rebels' final attack in what came to be called the Seven Days Campaign was easily repulsed at Malvern Hill.

McClellan was able to keep his army together and retreat without heavy losses. Nonetheless, Robert E. Lee's brilliant gamble had paid off. McClellan had been forced to fall back from his powerful position on Richmond's doorstep.

A partial retreat was not enough to suit Lee. McClellan still had a mighty army, and it was still camped too close to Richmond for Lee's comfort. Convinced that the best defense was a good offense, the Confederate leader decided to take another gamble. He was certain that if he could threaten the Northern capital, McClellan would be forced to scurry back to defend it. But Washington was well guarded by a reorganized army led by General John Pope. The Confederates did not have enough men to attack the North and defend Richmond at the same time.

The solution was to again violate the rules of military strategy by splitting the army. Stonewall Jackson's forces were sent north to challenge Pope's army, which was stationed southwest of Washington. Lee left a flimsy screen of troops to bar McClellan's path to Richmond and secretly marched a large segment of his men north to trap Pope.

McClellan could easily have wrecked the plan by advancing on Richmond. Lee would have been forced to scramble south to keep the Union troops from destroying the city. But as Lee had predicted, McClellan did not advance. In fact, as Lee's army pulled to the north, McClellan began to move in the same direction to join Pope's forces.

After several unsuccessful efforts to draw Pope into battle, Lee continued with the risk of a divided army. Jackson

Jeb Stuart (left) *and Stonewall Jackson* (below) *were two of Lee's most trusted and able lieutenants.*

was to attack Pope from the north, while Lee would quietly move in and strike from the south. Again, it was a race against time. Lee needed to defeat Pope before McClellan arrived and caught his divided forces. After a heroic display of marching stamina, Jackson's "foot cavalry" appeared at the rear of Pope's army near Bull Run Creek. Pope held a strong defensive position, however, and was able to hold off Jackson's furious strikes. While the outcome was still in doubt, Pope discovered thousands of fresh Confederate soldiers rushing into the battle.

For a time Pope's divisions held on bravely to their positions. The fighting grew so desperate that many of the Confederates ran out of ammunition and had to fight with bayonets—the blades affixed to their rifles. In the end, though, the Federals were driven from the field and retreated in disarray. Their collapse left a large Confederate army within striking distance of Washington, D.C., with nothing to bar its way. Hoping to prevent a humiliating ransacking of the nation's capital, McClellan withdrew his army completely into Northern territory and posed no further threat to Richmond.

Lee had performed an astounding feat. The newly named Army of Northern Virginia had not only rescued Richmond from a precarious situation but had also driven a mighty Yankee army back to its own doorstep.

The Seven Days Campaign and the routing of Pope at Bull Run instantly transformed Lee into a hero. The man who had been ridiculed as "Granny Lee" was suddenly being toasted as a military genius. Lee found this change most strange. Because of his strong religious convictions, Lee believed that humans had only a small influence on the events of history.

During the floundering campaign in western Virginia,

Northern and Southern forces clash at Bull Run.

this attitude had helped Lee shoulder criticism without complaint. There was no reason to give excuses or to blame others. All that Lee concerned himself with was doing his duty. He would let God decide the outcome. Nothing in the Seven Days Campaign or the Second Battle of Bull Run had changed that. Lee continued to do his duty to the best of his ability. The results had been more favorable this time, but he did not take credit for it.

Lee's firm belief that a just God was in control remained unshaken, even in the face of repeated misfortune. One of those bad breaks took place shortly after the defeat of Pope.

In September 1862, Lee decided to press his advantage over his shaken opponents by carrying the war to the North. He had several goals in mind as he crossed into Maryland. First, a series of Confederate successes on Northern soil might frighten the Northerners, who had never dreamed that their homes would be caught in the horrible crossfire of war. Perhaps this close-up look at battle would frighten them into abandoning the war effort. Second, the appearance of Southern troops in Maryland might encourage the many Confederate sympathizers who were known to live in that state. Finally,

Armies often constructed shallow trenches behind defensive walls or earthworks. Many soldiers lost their lives in the trenches.

moving the battleground into the North that autumn would allow Virginia farmers to harvest their crops in peace.

Lee's Army of Northern Virginia did stir up fear as it marched through the Maryland countryside. The troops did not get far, however. Expecting that the demoralized Federals would need time to regroup, Lee again split his force. Jackson was sent to capture the town of Harpers Ferry to the west, while the rest of the army moved north. But a copy of Lee's orders to his commanders was accidentally left behind when the Confederates broke camp one day. When Union soldiers happened on the camp, they found Lee's plan of attack.

General McClellan eagerly moved to take advantage of his luck. He could strike with confidence now that all uncertainty had been eliminated. He knew where Lee's army was and where it was going. Most importantly, he discovered that the Confederate force was not nearly as large as he had thought, and he realized just how vulnerable Lee's divided army was to attack.

"I have all the plans of the rebels, and will catch them in their own trap.... [I] will send you trophies," McClellan wrote to President Lincoln. McClellan boldly moved his army forward through the Catoctin Mountains. It was now Lee's army that was in danger of destruction. After staving off a Union attack at South Mountain, Lee retreated to Antietam Creek, near the town of Sharpsburg, Maryland, on September 17. All he could do was fight as hard as possible until reinforcements arrived from Harpers Ferry.

Murderous volleys of rifle and cannon fire swept across the fields. The Confederates fought off a series of Union attacks, but their losses were devastating. Lee's line of defense was growing desperately thin, and he constantly had to

Lee's forces suffered terrible losses at Antietam.

reshuffle his regiments to keep his line from breaking. Soldiers from the right flank raced behind the lines to defend the hard-pressed left. Lee risked weakening the center of his line in order to reinforce both flanks.

Thanks to Jackson's timely arrival from Harpers Ferry, the badly outnumbered Army of Northern Virginia managed to hold its ground against all attacks that day. But Lee saw that his position was hopeless. Casualties were gruesomely high, and those who had survived were exhausted. Lee had to pull back and try to get his battered force back to Virginia without further damage. Fortunately for Lee, McClellan reverted to his cautious nature and did not pursue the Confederates. This delay finally snapped Abraham Lincoln's patience with McClellan. "I said I would remove him if he let Lee's army get away from him, and I must do so," said Lincoln. The Union general was relieved of his command.

Lee was sorry to hear of McClellan's dismissal. "We always understood each other so well," he explained. "I fear they may continue to make these changes until they find someone I don't understand." But none of the Union generals who followed McClellan seemed to pose any greater mystery. Lee analyzed troop movements so skillfully that he could usually predict what any Union general was going to do. Rather than organize a long-term defensive strategy, Lee would simply play off his opponent. After watching the enemy approach, Lee would figure out what the Northern general was trying to do. He would then seize the offensive and take steps to ruin that plan.

Sometimes Lee so outmaneuvered his opponent that the result was almost an execution rather than a battle. A most glaring example of this came at the battle of Fredericksburg in December 1862. General Ambrose Burnside, who was selected to take McClellan's place at the head of the Army of the Potomac, was well aware that he was overmatched against Lee. He tried to decline the promotion, protesting that he was not capable of commanding such a large army. His pleas were ignored, and he reluctantly set out to fight Lee.

Any invasion of Virginia from the north required the crossing of a series of rivers that run southeast through the state. Burnside chose to cross the Rappahannock River near Fredericksburg. The high banks on the northern side of the river would provide cover for the crossing. Seeing that the lower land on the Fredericksburg side offered little natural defense, Lee offered only token resistance to the crossing. Most of his soldiers were positioned on higher ground a short way from the river. Jackson's infantry made another of their famous marches, 175 miles (280 km) in 12 days, to join Lee's defense.

When the Army of the Potomac reached the southern bank of the Rappahannock, they found entrenched Confederate forces staring down at them from the ridge. To reach the Confederates, the Union troops would have to dash uphill across a long, open field. The prospects did not look encouraging, but Burnside ordered his army to attack. Incredibly,

Lee outsmarted a string of Union generals including Ambrose Burnside.

they concentrated the main force of their attack against the Confederates' strongest position on Marye's Heights.

But their mission was hopeless. Lee's army wiped out the assault with only a quarter of his men taking part in the action. The first lines of attackers were beaten back with artillery fire. Burnside hurled wave after wave of infantry at the Confederates without coming close to breaching their walls. Rows of gray-coated Confederate soldiers loaded rifles and passed them to the their comrades in the front lines, who then fired into the close-packed Union ranks. By nightfall, the field was covered with dead Union soldiers, seven or eight deep in spots.

The sight of the slaughter of Union soldiers moved Lee to remark, "It is well that war is so terrible, else men would learn to love it too much." The hapless Burnside quickly retreated after suffering one of the worst defeats of the war.

Burnside was then replaced by General Joseph Hooker, a man known as "Fighting Joe." A fine organizer and strategist, Hooker was enormously popular with his men. Union morale was again high as the Army of the Potomac marched south for another try at the Army of Northern Virginia in the spring of 1863.

Hooker proved to be a far more sophisticated opponent than Burnside. Although he too sent some divisions to cross the river at Fredericksburg, he stretched his battlelines west to Chancellorsville. Hooker's forces outnumbered Lee's by roughly 140,000 to 60,000. By skillfully exploiting this advantage, Hooker soon had the Confederates in a dangerous position. Brimming with confidence, Hooker declared that "our enemy must either ingloriously fly or come out from behind his entrenchments and give us a battle on our own ground where certain destruction awaits him."

Lee appeared to have no choice but to retreat and wait for more favorable circumstances before giving battle. Defying the odds and the advice of some of his officers, Lee chose to do the opposite. Guessing that the Army of the Potomac would not repeat its earlier failure with a concentrated attack at Fredericksburg, Lee paid little attention to the 60,000 Union soldiers massed there under the command of General John Sedgwick. Instead, he predicted that the main attack would be aimed at Chancellorsville to the west.

Taking an outrageous risk, Lee split his army into three parts. General Jubal Early was left with only 10,000 men to hold Sedgwick at bay. Stonewall Jackson and 28,000 hard-marching foot soldiers then dashed around to attack Hooker's right side and rear. Lee attempted to battle the center of Hooker's army with only 18,000 men. Hooker was so stunned to learn that Lee was not retreating, but was actually attacking, that he lost his nerve. Despite his advantage in numbers and his reputation as "Fighting Joe," Hooker retreated from his favorable position. Confusion reigned at Union headquarters, and the outmanned Confederates easily drove the Federals from the field. Lee then regrouped and went after Sedgwick's divisions at Fredericksburg. Cut off from Hooker's aid, this division also suffered heavy losses and retreated back toward Washington.

Even in victory, though, Lee's army suffered. The brilliant Stonewall Jackson was riding near the front lines at Chancellorsville one night, surveying the enemy positions, when one of his own sentries fired on him. Jackson was hit three times. His left arm had to be amputated, and his chances for recovery were slim. When Lee heard the news, he sadly remarked that Jackson may have lost his left arm, but, by losing Jackson, "I have lost my right."

In 1863, President Lincoln issued the Emancipation Proclamation, freeing all slaves in the Confederacy.

Confederate general Jubal Early

The loss tested Lee's faith. He refused to believe that God would allow an accident to take his most reliable officer. Lee spent sleepless hours praying for Jackson's recovery. But a week later, Jackson died. Lee was devastated.

Despite Lee's success, the Confederate nation was slowly being drained of resources. While Lee did battle with Union forces in Virginia, other Confederate generals (including Joseph Johnston, now recovered from his wounds) were fighting west of the Appalachian Mountains. But the Confederate armies there were not holding up as well as Lee's forces in Virginia. In the West, Union armies led by General Ulysses

Grant were cutting deep into Southern lands. By the spring of 1863, Grant threatened to overwhelm the key Confederate stronghold at Vicksburg, Mississippi. Cut off from world trade by the Yankee naval blockade and lacking the industry to produce its own goods, the South began to run short of ammunition, clothing, and other supplies.

The South was also losing manpower. Death tolls were tremendous on both sides during the Civil War. As many as 25 percent of an army's soldiers might be killed, wounded, or captured during a major battle. Those who were wounded

Confederate soldiers play cards outside a tent at a temporary field encampment.

in action often died, even after surgery or amputation. Medicine was primitive by modern standards; infection took many lives. Disease swept through trenches and army encampments and killed many soldiers. Confederate and Union prisoners of war also died of disease and starvation in enemy prison camps. Deserters—soldiers who were no longer willing to fight—fled camp and reduced the ranks even further.

Both armies lost men in great numbers. But the North, simply because of its larger population, was able to draft and recruit new soldiers and reinforce its thinning ranks. Although sanitation and health care were poor in both armies, the Northern soldiers were better fed, better equipped, and far more numerous than their Southern opponents.

Lee had never believed that the South could win a prolonged war with the North. In the late spring of 1863 it was clear to him that the only way to end the war was to make the North lose its will to fight. Perhaps the mighty Army of Northern Virginia could break the North's spirit by winning a major battle on Northern soil. At any rate, goods were so scarce in the South that many of Lee's soldiers were without shoes. Lee could no longer find adequate food for his men and figured they would have a better chance of finding what they needed in the North.

EIGHT

Near Miss at Gettysburg

1863-1864

Historians have called Robert E. Lee the last of the "classic generals." He believed that war, horrible as it was, should remain a contest of cunning, strength, and courage. There were rules of etiquette to be followed to ensure that soldiers remained noble and honorable. Civilians on both sides were to be protected, laws were to be obeyed, courtesy to be extended. The modern concept of "total war" used by Northern generals such as Ulysses Grant and William Sherman was totally foreign to him. Fighting in the West, Grant and Sherman were willing to do whatever it took to win the war. Grant would sacrifice thousands of soldiers and accept individual defeats in the process of wearing down the South with his superior numbers. Sherman would destroy civilian property in an effort to reduce the enemy's ability to wage war.

As Lee marched north in the spring of 1863, he could have inflicted far more damage, and possibly panicked the

North, by torching the land and destroying property. But Lee would not fight that way. There was no burning and pillaging of private property as Lee marched toward Pennsylvania. His soldiers were under strict orders to raid federal Army supplies at will, but to leave the farmers alone. Those who ignored Lee's high standards did so at their own risk. Despite his kind, generous nature, Lee occasionally displayed such a raging temper that those who worked in the general's camp retained a healthy fear of him. Lee once had two soldiers executed for killing and robbing a farmer. Upon finding a straggler carrying a stolen pig, Lee ordered the man hanged —a sentence that was later reduced.

As Lee marched north through unfamiliar territory, he needed to know where the opposing army was and what it was doing. Lee relied on his cavalry to be his "eyes and ears," to gather this information.

Unfortunately, Lee's cavalry leader, Jeb Stuart, got carried away with the excitement of galloping through enemy lands. Instead of staying out of trouble and keeping Lee posted, Stuart got caught up in a skirmish with Union cavalry. Lee advanced through Maryland and into Pennsylvania, growing ever more unsure of his situation.

When Lee's advance regiments met some Union soldiers near the town of Gettysburg, Pennsylvania, Lee was not certain what he had run up against. More soldiers from each side arrived on the scene, and Lee was surprised to learn that he had encountered the main force of the Army of the Potomac, now led by General George Meade.

Gettysburg was at the hub of a number of important roads, and Lee had suspected that a battle might be fought there. But neither army had made plans for such a confrontation when the advance forces collided on July 1, 1863. Officers

Union soldiers periodically received new uniforms and equipment. The North, with its prosperous farms and factories, had an ample supply of food and materials, while the South suffered terrible shortages.

on each side had to follow their own instincts as it became obvious that a major battle could not be avoided. During the early stages of the battle, the advantage swung to the Confederates.

At this point, Lee sorely missed the presence of Stonewall Jackson. Following the general's death, Lee had reorganized the two corps of his Army of Northern Virginia into three corps. Pete Longstreet, slow and cautious, retained command of one corps. Jackson's former corps was divided between Richard Ewell and A. P. Hill. While the Confederates were pushing back the disorganized Union forces that had hastily assembled to meet them, Lee suggested that General Ewell fortify a section of high ground known as Culp's Hill.

Historians have said that one of Lee's weaknesses was his habit of giving suggestions rather than orders to his subordinates. His officers were free to use their own judgment to revise or even ignore his wishes. Many times, this worked to the Confederates' benefit. Stonewall Jackson had taken advantage of Lee's trust to fight aggressively and seize unexpected opportunities that would have been missed had he been bound by orders. But few officers were capable of matching Jackson's ability.

General Longstreet at Gettysburg

General George Meade

At Gettysburg, Lee's trust in his subordinates backfired. First Stuart had ridden off and taken his valuable cavalry out of the picture. Now Ewell chose not to follow up on Lee's directions, and this mistake strengthened the Union position. General Longstreet's corps got entangled with another column of Confederate troops, so it did not arrive when Lee expected and needed it.

More trouble followed. At almost the same time, both armies realized the strategic advantages of occupying a hill on the southern edge of the battlefield called Little Round Top. Lee ordered the position to be taken. But a squadron of Northerners reached the summit first. The Southerners could not dislodge the blue-coated Union soldiers, and the day ended with Meade's army in control of all the high ground along the battlefront. Despite sustaining horrible losses in a foolhardy charge through a wheat field, the Union forces held on to their advantage through the second day.

Up until this time, the Army of Northern Virginia had proved to be an almost unbeatable fighting machine. Its impressive streak of victories may have lured Lee into over-confidence. Lee's officers advised him to try to overturn the Yankees' southern flank. Instead Lee ordered a head-on assault of the center of the enemy line.

Lee, the gambler, was again taking a huge risk. The devastating amount of firepower available to each army made such open assaults nearly suicidal. The setup at Gettysburg was in some ways similar to what Burnside had encountered at Fredericksburg. The Confederates would have to charge across an open field into strong enemy defenses atop Cemetery Ridge. If they broke through, the Confederates would win a decisive victory. If not, defeat was inevitable. Either way, the price in dead and maimed soldiers would be frightful.

General George Pickett's division was selected to make the fateful charge. After Confederate artillery shelled the Northern positions with every piece of ammunition available, Pickett's infantry surged forward. A long line of 15,000 gray-uniformed soldiers hurled themselves into the cannon and musket fire from Cemetery Ridge.

Lee watched the desperate scene unfold with a mixture of horror and awe. While their comrades were falling on all sides of them, a small group of Confederates drove into the Union line and broke through the main line of defense. Historians have called this the "high water mark" of the Confederacy. From this point on, the fortunes of the South declined steadily.

The men who had broken through the Union line came under crossfire from Union reserves. With no reinforcements to support their assault, the Confederate soldiers were beaten back. As all through the battle of Gettysburg, the Confederate battle plan was not well coordinated. Too few attackers survived the murderous volleys from Cemetery Ridge. Pickett's Charge ended in failure.

"I never saw troops behave more magnificently than Pickett's division of Virginians did today in that grand charge," Lee said. "And if they had been supported as they were to have been...we would have held that position, and the day would have been ours. Too bad! Too bad!" Lee's shattered army was now in danger of being totally destroyed.

General Meade made no effort to pursue the wounded Confederate army. Few men had ever gotten the best of Lee in battle, and Meade was content to quit while his weary

Over 600,000 soldiers died during the Civil War. Not all soldiers died in battle, however. Many died of disease.

army was ahead. The Confederates limped back toward Virginia. When they reached the swollen Potomac River at the border of the Confederacy, Lee sat sadly atop his horse Traveller and waited until every soldier had safely crossed.

Even for the self-disciplined Lee, this time it was not enough that he had tried his best. General Lee accepted the entire blame for the Confederate defeat and submitted his resignation to President Jefferson Davis. He did not criticize any of his subordinates. But long after the battle, he once confided to a friend, "If I had had Stonewall Jackson with me, so far as man can see, I should have won the battle of Gettysburg."

NINE

Marse Robert and the Lost Cause

1864-1865

Lee's resignation was not accepted. The defeat did nothing to tarnish his reputation among the troops. But with the disaster at Gettysburg, the dream of an independent Confederate nation slowly began to fade. President Lincoln brought in his toughest commander, Ulysses Grant, to lead the Union armies against the legendary Bobby Lee. Grant's relentless style of attack had worn away Confederate resistance in the West. Realizing that the Southerners were nearing the end of their manpower and supplies, Grant's plan was to force them to use both. Lee could continue to win his battles, but sooner or later, his army would be exhausted.

While Robert E. Lee earned his distinction as a military genius in the battles of 1862 and 1863, it was his performance in the later years of the Civil War, 1864 and 1865, that set him apart as a legend. By the sheer force of his character, Lee inspired a ragged army of men to fight far past the point at which most would have given up.

Lee himself was mystified by the effect that he had on his soldiers. But it was no mystery to those around him. Even during a savage war the general shone as an example of honor and decency. The Confederate soldiers saw in General Lee all the best qualities of the Southern society that they were fighting for—honor, courtesy, and generosity. The noble stature of Robert E. Lee seemed to offer proof that, whatever misfortune might befall them, their cause was just.

It was easy to fight for a general who acted more like a father than a superior officer. There was no question that "Marse (master) Robert," as his soldiers were fond of calling him, was absolutely in charge. Yet he avoided the temptation to use power for personal advantage. The Lee headquarters was no kingly palace. While it was customary for officers to set up headquarters in a house near the army's encampment, Lee pitched a tent alongside the rest of the soldiers. He demanded no pomp or luxury. In fact, soldiers often walked through Lee's tent grounds without realizing the area was occupied by the commander of their army. Only in the final year of the war, when Lee's once-vital health had been sapped, did he consent to put his headquarters in a house.

It was easy for soldiers to fight for a general who genuinely loved his men. Robert E. Lee was not ashamed to let the tears flow when he heard of the deaths of colleagues such as Stonewall Jackson. In the spring of 1864, a contingent of Longstreet's men returned to the Army of Northern Virginia after having fought alongside Confederate armies in Tennessee. Lee rode out to meet these frazzled soldiers as they arrived. Out of respect for their valiant efforts in that losing campaign, Lee removed his hat as the soldiers rode by. That gesture of concern so moved the men that they put aside their frustrations and cheered.

The once-proud Confederate soldiers were starving and ragged by war's end. But inspired by "Marse Robert," they continued to fight.

Lee's soldiers bore miserable conditions, but they knew that their middle-aged general was voluntarily accepting the same hardships. Lee could not bear to be served a full meal while his soldiers had to subsist on meager rations. As food became more and more scarce, General Lee cut back his portions accordingly. One Christmas, a large box of turkeys was delivered to the high-ranking officers of the army, courtesy of the Confederate government. As the commanding officer, Lee was given the largest turkey. The general immediately ordered that it be given to the wounded in a nearby hospital, and his junior officers did the same.

In mid-December of 1864, Lee was summoned back to Richmond for urgent meetings with President Davis. By this time, Lee's family had been driven from its home at Arlington and was living in Richmond. It had been five years since Lee had been with his family on Christmas, and many of Lee's officers were certain that he would take this opportunity to do so.

One of Lee's closest aides disagreed. Even though no one would have begrudged Lee this well-earned holiday at home, the aide predicted Lee would probably ride back to camp on the eve of the holiday. Sure enough, Lee appeared at the Confederate camp just a few days before Christmas.

Despite the killing and destruction that surrounded his campaign, Lee strove to follow high standards of human conduct. He never criticized or spoke in anger of the forces arrayed against him. In fact, it was not until late in the conflict, in the midst of the total war campaigns of Grant and Sherman, that Lee regularly referred to the Union armies as "the enemy."

Lee kept his men focused on his vision of honor and duty. Late in the war, one of his generals, E. P. Alexander, suggested that the Confederates disband their large armies and turn to guerrilla warfare. This strategy of going into hiding, making surprise attacks, and disappearing into the countryside had proven effective for many armies that did not have the strength to face a superior enemy in open battle.

Lee, however, referred to guerrilla war as "bushwhacking." He foresaw that such an army would grow lawless.

General Lee filled his soldiers with both fear and awe.

General Grant (left) *was a fierce soldier who refused to let up in his pursuit of Lee's army.*

"The men would be without rations and under no control of officers," he said. "They would be compelled to rob and steal in order to live. . . . We would bring on a state of affairs it would take the country years to recover from."

Lee's gentle argument was more than persuasive. General Alexander admitted that Lee had "answered my suggestion from a plane so far above it, that I was ashamed of having made it."

The regular soldiers of the Army of Northern Virginia knew how Alexander felt. A lively topic of discussion among the soldiers for a time was Charles Darwin's newly published theory of evolution. While the men were debating the possibilities that humans were descended from apes, one Confederate soldier summed up the feeling about their commander-in-chief. The soldier did not doubt that he and all his companions could have evolved from apes, "but I tell you none less than God could have made such a man as Marse Robert."

Lee's soldiers were so devoted to him that many valued Lee's life more than their own. On two occasions during the fighting, when the Confederate situation seemed desperate, General Lee attempted to repulse the Union attackers himself. On both occasions, his soldiers threw themselves into the path of his horse, grabbed its reins, and refused to let him advance. "Go back, General Lee! Go back! We won't go on unless you go back!" they shouted.

When Ulysses S. Grant took charge of the Army of the Potomac in March of 1864, he found that Lee's reputation for greatness had nearly paralyzed the North's war effort. At one point, Grant cried out in frustration that he was getting tired of hearing so much about what Lee was going to do. He suggested to his officers that they spend more time thinking about what *they* were going to do.

It did not take long for Grant to discover that the tales about Lee were more than just legend. In May Grant began yet another advance on the Confederate capital of Richmond. Following Grant's movements closely, Lee was able to predict where the Union forces were headed. While Grant's army was trying to work its way through a tangled mass of forest and thickets known simply as "the Wilderness," Lee hurled a surprise attack at him. The vegetation was so thick that organized plans of attack and defense broke down quickly. "Much hard fighting ensued," wrote Lee's aide Walter Taylor. "For two days there was a murderous wrestle; severe and rapid blows were given and received in turn, until sheer exhaustion called a truce."

But even though the Union forces sustained heavy losses, Grant did not panic. Not only did his men fight their way out of the Wilderness to safety, they did what the Army of the Potomac had never done before. Instead of retreating after a defeat, they continued attacking. The North had finally found a general who was not intimidated by Lee. Grant was willing to accept a setback as long as he could keep pushing forward with his 120,000-man army.

Lee's force by this time numbered fewer than 60,000 men. His options were also limited by the fact that he was tied to Richmond. The Confederacy had made a major error in locating its capital in that city, within easy reach of the Union armies. To protect the city, Lee had to keep his army in the narrow space between Richmond and the Army of the Potomac. He wasn't able to maneuver at will.

Less than a week after the furious battle in the Wilderness, the two forces met again at Spotsylvania Court House, just south of Fredericksburg. The fighting there was so fierce that one Union general reported that they had shot down a forest as well as the enemy. Grant continued to move south, but Lee refused to back down. A few weeks later, Grant tried another frontal assault on Lee's position at Cold Harbor, just outside of Richmond.

This attack was every bit as doomed as the run up Marye's Heights at Fredericksburg. Confederate defenders fired on the attacking troops from trenches. Union soldiers were mowed down in such numbers (7,000 were killed or wounded) that some appalled Northerners labeled Grant "the Butcher."

Even though he had made a serious mistake, Grant kept pushing toward Richmond. Lee realized that Grant would not be scared off. The only way to stop the Army of the Potomac was to destroy it.

Reluctant to be drawn into further futile assaults and unable to maneuver his way past Lee into Richmond, Grant decided to go at it from the south. If he could swing around and capture the town of Petersburg, an important rail center, both Lee and Richmond would be cut off from supplies.

Lee, again analyzing the situation correctly, rushed troops to the south and threw up defensive works before the Federals could attack. Grant refused to attempt another attack, and he dug in for a more cautious confrontation. Both armies constructed earthworks within sight of each other and waited.

Lee realized that there was not much he could hope to accomplish on this battlefield. While Grant could draw on fresh troops to replace his casualties, Lee's numbers were dwindling. He had been fighting with every man available. He had not been able to spare any for a reserve force. Although Lee's men loved him dearly, many could no longer bear the hunger and misery in the trenches. Thousands deserted and headed home. A long siege would not hurt Grant's well-stocked army, but Lee's poorly supplied men could not survive much longer.

The South's only hope was to outlast the North's patience. Many Northerners, appalled by the high casualty figures from the Army of the Potomac, were losing their desire to continue the war.

As Lee's lines of defense were stretched ever thinner, he decided to use his old tactic of striking at Washington, D.C. He hoped this would draw some Union troops away from

Richmond and ease pressure on the entrenched Confederate army. Lee sent General Jubal Early and 20,000 soldiers racing northward. After some initial successes in the Shenandoah Valley, Early advanced to the outskirts of Washington. But he did not have enough of an army to do serious damage. In October 1864, Early was defeated at the hands of General Phil Sheridan.

In the meantime, Lee held out at Petersburg all through the summer, fall, and winter against a variety of probes and skirmishes. It was a valiant but futile defense.

The Confederate armies in the West were faring even worse. First General Joseph Johnston and later General John

Both armies dug trenches and built defensive works that extended for miles around cities such as Atlanta, Georgia (above), and Petersburg, Virginia.

Hood tried to hold off William Sherman's Union army as it advanced through Georgia. But Sherman took Atlanta and torched the city. He proceeded to destroy railroads, farms, and towns as he marched south toward Savannah. Sherman's victory revived the North's spirits. There was no hope that the pressure against Lee would be relieved.

In the spring of 1865, Grant broke down the right flank of Lee's thin, brittle line of defense. Petersburg was lost and Richmond along with it.

"Well, gentlemen, what shall we do?" Lee asked, as he always did when he wrestled with a difficult problem. As usual, he did not expect anyone to answer the question for him. The responsibility was his. By this time, Lee had grown weary in body and spirit. He was racked with fevers and blood poisoning.

Instead of abandoning his spiritual convictions, though, Lee leaned on them as heavily as ever. He still believed that the outcome of his struggle was in the hands of a higher authority. He believed as strongly as ever in doing his duty to the best of his ability and accepting whatever might result without complaint. But he had begun to despair of finding any contentment or peace in his life. Hearing of the death of General A. P. Hill, Lee responded, "He is at rest now, and we who are left are the ones to suffer."

With deserters reducing his strength to only 35,000 ragged fighting men, Lee determined that his only hope was to try to join General Johnston, who now had command of a small army in North Carolina. The odds against him were great. Union forces were now three times his strength. All Lee could do was try to reach some supplies at the town of Amelia Court House to the west and then escape from Grant's trap.

Federal cavalry, however, had been active in the area.
Train tracks were torn up, and Confederate provisions had
been captured. When Lee arrived at Amelia, the supplies
were not there. With no food and nearly surrounded by Grant's
huge armies, Lee and his soldiers seemed to be in a hopeless
position.

William Sherman (opposite) *marched through Georgia, destroying cities, farms, and railroads like this one outside of Atlanta.*

Yet Lee refused to give in to despair. During one march he quietly scolded a young soldier for not having one of his trouser legs tucked into his boot. It was important, Lee told his soldiers, not to give any appearance of being demoralized. They were still the Army of Northern Virginia, one of the finest collections of fighting men ever assembled, and he did not want them to forget it.

During the next five days, Lee made every effort to break out of the grip of the enemy. But Grant was not about to let him escape. Every move was thwarted by the North's overwhelming numbers. Lee attempted one last breakout maneuver, sending General John Gordon's men against the Union cavalry that blocked the only possible line of escape. If Gordon could punch out there, the army could stream through the hole into North Carolina.

For a time it seemed as though it would work. Gordon's troops broke through the Federal ranks. As they did so, however, a large contingent of blue-coated infantry arrived on the scene. Gordon pleaded for reinforcements, but Lee had none to send.

During this final week, Lee could hardly bring himself to consider the possibility of surrender. He would rather have died in a last hopeless battle than give up. "What would the country think of me?" he asked one of his officers.

"There is no country," the man replied. "There has been no country, General, for a year or more. You are the country to these men. They have fought for you.... Without pay or clothes, or care of any sort, their devotion to and faith in you have been the only thing which has held this army together." The remaining soldiers were so devoted to Lee that they would keep fighting as long as he gave the word. But their position was hopeless. To ask the men to keep fighting would be the equivalent of ordering them to their deaths.

For Lee, it was a matter of choosing between conflicting obligations. Should he fight for his cause to the end, or should he carry out his duty to his men who had already fought and suffered so much?

In the end, Lee's sense of responsibility to his soldiers won out over the humiliation of defeat. He saw finally that the question was not "What will the country think?" but "What is right?" If surrendering the army was the best course of action, then he would do it, regardless of what anyone thought of him.

Charleston, South Carolina, in 1865. By war's end, many Southern cities were in ruins and would have to be rebuilt.

On April 9, 1865, Robert E. Lee donned his best suit, mounted Traveller, and rode into the tiny town of Appomattox Court House. There, at the house of Wilmer McLean, he met Ulysses Grant and surrendered his army. This left only Johnston's army in the field for the Confederates. Johnston would surrender later that month.

At Appomattox, the two enemies put the past behind them and began the work of easing the pain of a country that had already suffered enough.

There was no jubilation among the Union leaders, no sense of superiority, no vindictiveness about defeating an army that had killed so many of their comrades. Grant and his generals admired the skillful, honorable way in which Lee had carried out his duty. The North's commander paid tribute to the valor of the Army of Northern Virginia by offering generous terms of surrender.

"I take it that most of the men in the [Confederate] ranks are small farmers," Grant said, "and as the country has been so raided by the two armies, it is doubtful whether they will be able to put in a crop to carry themselves and their families through the next winter without the aid of the horses they are now riding. . . . I will instruct the officers. . . . to let all the men who claim to own a horse or mule take the animals home with them to work their little farms."

Lee conducted himself with his usual politeness and dignity. As Lee mounted his horse and departed, Grant and his aides silently removed their hats in a last tribute to their enemy.

Lee's own troops were equally reverent. Some of his soldiers insisted they could still fight. They were stunned that Lee had surrendered. Lee fought back tears as he explained, "Men, we have fought the war together, and I have done the best I could for you."

Other soldiers crowded around and told the defeated general how much he meant to them. "God bless you, Marse Robert," they said. In the midst of this bitter moment, a throng of ragged Confederates parted before the general and cheered as he rode past.

Lee's brief farewell statement summed up his philosophy of life. After generously praising his men, Lee said, "You will take with you the satisfaction that proceeds from the consciousness of duty faithfully performed."

Although it pained him to linger at the scene of his defeat, Lee stayed until the federal army paroled all of his men: They were allowed to return to their homes in exchange for a promise not to fight. Then Lee set off on Traveller to return to his family, now living in Richmond. As he rode through the streets of that burned and defeated city, word of his arrival passed quickly. Despite his surrender, Lee was treated like a hero. Crowds gathered to watch the general go into his home and lay down his sword, never to take it up again.

The Lees' home in Richmond. Arlington was confiscated by federal troops and was later made into a national cemetery.

TEN

A Beacon of Hope

1865-1870

Much of the South lay in ruins, and many of its young men lay in their graves. Through a program called Reconstruction, the federal government set out to readmit the Confederate states into the Union, restore the Southern economy, protect the rights of the newly freed blacks, and pardon the Southern people. Like many who had served the Confederate cause, Lee struggled to find hope for the future. But for a time he could do little but sit around in stunned silence.

Lee understood that he was a symbol to the South. The Southern people still looked to him for leadership. Robert E. Lee had to show that defeat was not the end of the world. The conflict had to be put behind, and the South, ravaged by war, had to be rebuilt.

But what could a tired, 58-year-old defeated army officer do? He had devoted his career to the military and now that career was over. Lee was still loved by his followers. But he had been a military leader of an open rebellion against the United States government. He realized that any public appearances he made would arouse impassioned memories of the war. Wishing to avoid controversy, Lee refused to make such appearances.

Some people suggested that Lee could contribute a great deal by writing. Lee still believed, as did many Southern leaders, that the states had numerous rights that the federal government should not attempt to take away. What better person to plead the South's cause than the eloquent general?

Ironically, though, the well-spoken Lee stumbled badly in his efforts to write. Although he spent a good deal of time assembling documents, he was never able to produce an account of any of his Civil War campaigns.

The federal government had confiscated the property at Arlington, and the Lees had little money left. There were many offers of help, and Lee could have lived well had he taken advantage of just a few of them. But he politely declined in every case. An insurance company, realizing that Lee's name was a synonym for integrity, offered him a salary of $50,000 for doing practically nothing. Lee did not even consider it.

In August 1865, a group of college officials made Lee a modest offer. To some, the invitation seemed so ridiculous that the group was almost embarrassed to approach the general. Would the illustrious Robert E. Lee be interested in taking over tiny Washington College in Lexington, Virginia? It was hardly a prestigious position. The place was nearly bankrupt and had dwindled to only four professors and 40 students!

Even though he had not had a positive experience as a school administrator at West Point, Lee accepted the post that many thought was below his dignity. The manner of

Lee's sons Rooney (left) and Custis (below) both served as generals in the Confederate army. Custis succeeded his father as president of Washington College.

Tiny Washington College would eventually become a prestigious Southern university.

work lent its own dignity, Lee explained. The South needed to focus on the future. By educating youth, Lee might be able to make a small difference in helping to rebuild a shattered country. "Now, more than at any other time, Virginia and every other state in the South needs us. We must try and, with as little delay as possible, go to work to build up their prosperity," he said.

President Lee brought the same measure of grace and integrity to Washington College (now Washington and Lee University) that he had carried into all his pursuits. He lived simply in Lexington with his wife and three surviving daughters and refused any displays of pomp and ceremony. Neither his meager salary nor his numerous duties prompted a complaint. As at West Point, Lee took extreme interest in the progress of his students. Those who did poorly came under particularly close scrutiny. The gentle prodding of one of the South's most respected persons rarely failed to motivate them. Lee frequently visited classrooms and even provided space in his own house for a poor student who had nowhere else to study.

While he hated to punish students, he would not tolerate disrespect. On one occasion, he told a student visiting his office to remove his chewing tobacco. When the student returned to the office, still chewing his wad, Lee wrote out a letter expelling the student from the school.

Under Lee's guidance, the college's finances improved, and enrollment surpassed 400. During these years, Lee faithfully lived up to his role as a model for the South. He was pleasant and cheerful around family and friends. Although he tried to avoid public places, he courteously accepted the visits of thousands of well-wishers.

Lee refused to submit to hatred or bitterness, even though he suffered more abuse than did many Confederates. The federal government's Reconstruction program offered pardons to all but the major Confederate leaders. Northerners who were not as forgiving as General Grant once tried to indict Lee for treason. Devoted Confederates denounced him for applying for a special pardon from President Andrew Johnson. In 1868, Lee asked the government to return some of his wife's family heirlooms that had once belonged to George Washington. These items had been confiscated when Arlington was taken over as a federal post. The Johnson administration was prepared to return the heirlooms until some congressmen got word of the action. Declaring that it would be an insult to hand over George Washington's property to a Rebel general, Congress refused the request.

Lee (seated, second from left) and other former Confederate leaders gather at White Sulpher Springs, North Carolina. Unlike most Southerners, the Confederate commanders were not pardoned by the federal government.

Despite such treatment, Lee declared that he had never known a moment of bitterness or resentment and that it saddened him to see it in others. Concerning Washington's heirlooms, he commented, "I hope the possessors appreciate them and may imitate the example of their original owner.... In this way, they will accomplish some good to the country."

While his public attitude was always positive and hopeful, the burdens and sorrows of Lee's life weighed heavily upon him in private. He could not rid himself of a sense of failure. "I much enjoy the charms of civil life and find too late that I have wasted the best years of my existence," he said. The depression that had periodically visited him throughout his career stayed with him until the end.

Lee's health began to decline in 1869. In late September of 1870, after walking home from a meeting in a cold rain, Lee collapsed in exhaustion. Two weeks later, on October 12, 1870, Lee died. His last official act had been to contribute the needed funds to provide a salary for a church worker.

On the final day of his command of the Army of Northern Virginia, Lee had predicted that history would judge him harshly for the surrender of his army in the field. In this he could not have been more mistaken. Historians have universally praised Robert E. Lee. The fact that he fought for a losing cause in no way diminished the qualities that set him above his contemporaries.

Perhaps the reason for this may be found in a more accurate prediction that Lee once made. In April 1865, as he faced the inevitable surrender, Lee was heard to comment that in a few days it would all be ended just as he had expected it to from the very beginning.

In other words, Lee had been quite certain all along that Virginia's cause was hopeless. Despite this, he never wavered in his devotion to his first loyalty. While he may have rued his choice of a military career, not for a moment did he regret his decision to decline the United States Army command in favor of fighting for Virginia. Robert E. Lee stood for the values that he believed to be worth far more than success, security, or wealth: "the glory of duty done, the honor of the integrity of principle." In defending those values, Lee never lost a battle.

For Further Reading

BOOKS ABOUT ROBERT E. LEE

Schlesinger, Arthur M., ed. *Robert E. Lee: Confederate General*. New York: Chelsea House, 1989.

Weidhorn, Manfred. *Robert E. Lee*. New York: Atheneum, 1988.

BOOKS ABOUT THE CIVIL WAR

Carter, Alden R. *The Battle of Gettysburg*. New York: Franklin Watts, 1990.

Meltzer, Milton. *Voices from the Civil War*. New York: Thomas Y. Crowell, 1989.

Murphy, Jim. *The Boys' War: Confederate and Union Soldiers Talk About the Civil War*. New York: Clarion Books, 1990.

Welsh, Douglas. *The Civil War*. London: Bison Books Limited, 1982.

BOOKS ABOUT CIVIL WAR LEADERS

Freedman, Russell. *Lincoln: A Photobiography*. New York: Houghton Mifflin, 1987.

Fritz, Jean. *Stonewall*. New York: Putnam Publishing Group, 1979.

Viola, Herman J. *Ulysses S. Grant*. New York: Chelsea House, 1990.

BOOKS ABOUT SLAVERY

Evitts, William J. *Captive Bodies, Free Spirits: The Story of Southern Slavery*. New York: Julian Messner, 1985.

Graham, Lorenz. *John Brown: A Cry for Freedom*. New York: Thomas Y. Crowell, 1980.

Index

Quoted passages are reprinted from the following:

pp. 66, 98 (2nd): *Lee and Grant*. Gene Smith. New York: McGraw-Hill, 1984.

pp. 11 (1st), 18: Smith citing *The Life of General Robert Edward Lee*. Emily V. Mason. Baltimore: John Murphy, 1874.

p. 11 (2nd): Smith citing *Lincoln and His Generals*. T. Harry Williams. New York: Alfred A. Knopf, 1952.

pp. 26 (1st), 41 (both), 42, 44, 46, 47, 55, 70, 82, 88 (both), 89 (1st), 93, 98 (1st), 99, 104, 106 (1st): *Lee*. Douglas Southall Freeman. New York: Charles Scribner's Sons, 1961.

p. 26 (2nd): Smith citing *R.E. Lee*. Vol. 1. Douglas Southall Freeman. New York: Charles Scribner's Sons, 1934-35.

p. 29: Smith citing *Robert E. Lee*. Margaret Sanborn. Philadelphia and New York: J.B. Lippincott, 1966.

pp. 33 (2nd), 48, 51: *The Marble Man: Robert E. Lee and His Image in American Society*. Thomas Connelly. New York: Alfred A. Knopf, 1977.

p. 33 (1st): Connelly citing "The Military Education of Robert E. Lee." Eben Swift. *Virginia Magazine of History and Biography* (April 1929).

pp. 56, 89 (2nd): Smith citing *Military Memoirs of a Confederate*. E. P. Alexander. New York: Charles Scribner's Sons, 1907.

p. 65: *Lincoln Finds a General*. Vol. 1. Kenneth P. Williams. New York: Doubleday, 1949.

p. 67: Smith citing *Jeb Stuart*. Burke Davis. New York: Rinehart, 1957.

p. 69 (1st): Smith citing *General Lee*. Fitzhugh Lee. New York: Fawcett Publications, 1961.

p. 69 (2nd): *Meade of Gettysburg*. Freeman Cleaves. Norman: University of Oklahoma Press, 1980.

p. 81: *Witness to Gettysburg*. Richard Wheeler. New York: Harper & Row, 1987.

p. 90: *My Four Years with General Lee*. Walter Taylor. Bloomington: Indiana University Press, 1962.

p. 96: Smith citing *The End of an Era*. John S. Wise. New York: Houghton Mifflin, 1900.

pp. 106 (2nd), 107: Smith citing *Personal Reminiscences, Anecdotes, and Letters of General Robert E. Lee*. William J. Jones. New York: Doubleday, 1874.